REDISCOVERING SPIRITUAL *Warfare*

HOW TO BATTLE AND WIN AGAINST THE UNSEEN ENEMY
VOLUME I

REDISCOVERING SPIRITUAL *Warfare*

HOW TO BATTLE AND WIN AGAINST THE UNSEEN ENEMY
VOLUME I

KEVIN BAILEY

TOUCH OF THE MASTER PUBLISHING

INDIANAPOLIS

Rediscovering Spiritual Warfare: How to Battle and Win Against the Unseen Enemy

Published by Touch of the Master Publishing
P.O. Box 533128
Indianapolis, IN 46253
www.touchofthemasterhmi.org

Queries regarding rights and permissions should be addressed to: Touch of the Master Publishing at touchofthemaster888@yahoo.com.

Unless otherwise noted, all Scripture quotations are taken from the Holy Bible, NEW KING JAMES VERSION®. Copyright© 1982 by Thomas Nelson, Inc. Used by permission. All rights reserved.

Scriptures marked KJV are taken from the KING JAMES VERSION (KJV): KING JAMES VERSION, public domain.

Scriptures marked NAS are taken from the New American Standard Bible®, Copyright © 1960, 1962, 1963, 1968, 1972, 1973, 1975, 1977, 1995 by The Lockman Foundation. Used by permission.

Scriptures marked NIV are taken from the NEW INTERNATIONAL VERSION (NIV): Scripture taken from THE HOLY BIBLE, NEW INTERNATIONAL VERSION ®. Copyright©1973, 1978, 1984, 2011 by Biblica, Inc.™. Used by permission of Zondervan.

ISBN: 978-0-578-65776-9

Interior design by Arlana Johnson

Cover design by
Flaming Sword Productions
Shirri Buchanan
flamingswordwitty@gmail.com

20 21 22 23 24 — 9 8 7 6 5 4 3 2 1

Printed in the United States of America

DEDICATION

To Kalyn K. Bailey

You will carry the torch of the Apostolic, deliverance, and
spiritual warfare throughout the world
and unto many generations.

ACKNOWLEDGMENTS

Thank you to everyone who encouraged and support-ed me in the writing of this book. God bless you all.

I am grateful to Apostle Kim Muniz who spent many hours typing and bringing order to the content.

Many thanks to Elder Toni Thompson, who endured warfare throughout this process, and for recovering the information for this book that we thought was lost.

A big thank you to Arlana Johnson for the countless hours dedicated to making this book become a reality.

Thank you to Apostle Ricky and Prophetess Deandrea Thomas for believing in me and encouraging me to write this book. Thank you also to Apostle Mario and Prophetess Joyce Lopez—you both have a special place in my heart.

TABLE OF CONTENTS

FOREWORD

Rediscovering Spiritual Warfare: How to Battle and Win Against the Unseen Enemy by Apostle Kevin Bailey is a tool for spiritual warfare filled with foundational principles based upon strong scriptural insight. Through intercession, decrees, and understanding the weapons God has given us, Apostle Bailey demonstrates how we can defeat the enemy.

Truly, this book teaches us that we are "God's Battle Axes and Weapons of War" (Jeremiah 51:20). This book excites me because its style is based upon executing judgments, as written in Psalm 149:9.

Apostle Dr. Ivory Hopkins
a.k.a. The General of Deliverance
Overseer and Founder
Pilgrims Ministry of Deliverance
Georgetown, DE

INTRODUCTION

You are in a war! Whether you know it or not, you have been enlisted in the army of God as a soldier of Jesus Christ. At any time, you can be on the verge of battle with your enemies. If you choose to not engage, you will become a casualty of war. But, if you stand and fight, all of heaven—including God Himself—is available to lead you into victory.

> And he shall say to them, 'Hear, O Israel: Today you are on the verge of battle with your enemies. Do not let your heart faint, do not be afraid, and do not tremble or be terrified because of them; for the LORD your God is He who goes with you, to fight for you against your enemies, to save you.'
>
> —Deuteronomy 20:3-4

> O GOD the Lord, the strength of my salvation, You have covered my head in the day of battle.
>
> —Psalm 140:7

> ...A time to love, and a time to hate; a time of war, and a time of peace.
>
> —Ecclesiastes 3:8

One of the biggest deceptions in the body of Christ is around spiritual warfare. In the Greek language, the word for warfare is *strateia*, which means military service.[1] Warfare also is defined as military operations between enemies, or struggle between competing entities. Similar terms include battle, conflict, combat, and hostile clash of arms. Simply put, spiritual warfare is fighting against the devil and his cohorts. It is waged in the spirit—the unseen realm. The enemy operates undercover to keep the saints of God ignorant to the truth about spiritual warfare. He cloaks it in mystery, attempts to discredit it, and instigates fear to make believers avoid it at all costs.

As a result, many see it as unnecessary or intimidating. And those who do engage in it, often are ineffective due to lack of preparation and poor execution. This is why, even after deliverance, many Christians remain bound by poverty, infirmity, mental illness, the effects of trauma, generational curses, and a host of other issues. They are oppressed, depressed, bewitched, tormented, and ultimately held back from fulfilling their God-appointed destinies. For every believer, engaging in spiritual warfare is essential to breaking bondages. I wrote the first volume of *Rediscovering Spiritual Warfare: How to Battle and Win Against the Unseen Enemy* for this very reason. It is time to encourage, instruct, and equip the saints for battle as Christ's good soldiers.

> Proclaim this among the nations:
> "Prepare for war!
> Wake up the mighty men,
> Let all the men of war draw near,
> Let them come up."
>
> —Joel 3:9

> "You are My battle-ax and weapons of war:
> For with you I will break the nation in pieces;
> With you I will destroy kingdoms;
> With you I will break in pieces the horse and its rider;
> With you I will break in pieces the chariot and its rider..."
>
> —Jeremiah 51:20-21

He teaches my hands to make war, so that my arms
can bend a bow of bronze.

—Psalm 18:34

This book was birthed out of almost 15 years of my experience as an intercessor. As an Apostle, I am committed to a life-long career in spiritual warfare. My mandate is to war against principalities, demonic networks, spiritual wickedness, and man-made traditions that impact individuals and territories. What I have written in this book is based on proven spiritual warfare strategies, guided by the Holy Spirit and the Word of God. I have traveled to more than 30 cities, regions, and nations, employing the same approaches, prayers and decrees that I will share with you. And I have personally witnessed the freedom, healing, and miracles that have come through warring (you can read about some of these experiences later in the book). It is my prayer that as you read, you will receive revelation from God and be equipped to:

- Establish a solid foundation for engaging in warfare.

- Identify, understand, and use your weapons.
- Understand how to configure your weapons.
- Know your enemy and his strategies.
- Prepare yourself ahead of battle.
- Effectively engage in battle using prayers and decrees.

To bring clarity and revelation, I have incorporated many supporting scriptures throughout this book. I encourage you to have your Bible ready to reference as you read, so that you can highlight, review, and meditate on key scriptures as you are led. Doing this will help to undergird and strengthen you, as you begin to understand more about spiritual warfare and how to battle in the unseen realm.

The enemy did his best to deter and frustrate the completion of this project. My ministry team, Touch of the Master Healing Ministries International, and others, were in constant prayer and intercession. We experienced our share of warfare and attacks throughout the process, but nearly everyone who supported and read this book received healing, deliverance, and breakthrough. I am believing the same for you, your family, congregants, and those to whom you minister. So, let's prepare for battle, get ready to engage, and fight!

SALVATION THROUGH JESUS CHRIST

You must understand that the strategies in this book only are effective if you are a follower of Jesus Christ; that is, if you believe in the death, burial and resurrection of the Lord Jesus. If you have not yet made the decision to become a Christian, I encourage you to do so now (see Salvation Prayer on page 107). Don't delay. God loves you so much that He gave His only Son, Jesus, that whomever believes in Him would live forever (see John 3:16). God has a destiny already in place for your life and all of His plans are designed to make you prosper and give you hope (see Jeremiah 1:5, 29:11).

Chapter 1

ESTABLISHING YOUR FOUNDATION FOR SPIRITUAL WARFARE

Training for battle starts with intense preparation. In the U.S. Army, all recruits begin with a 10-week basic training period (also referred to as boot camp). This process is designed to de-civilize you. Becoming a soldier means abandoning your former way of life. Training begins in the classroom where you learn how to conduct yourself with new rules, regulations, and policies. The next several weeks is an immersion into military life, with guidance from your Drill Sergeant. He or she puts you in the field to get you into top mental and physical condition and build your endurance. Eventually you are ready to become a marksman. You receive a standard-issued M16A2 weapon and learn how to shoot from different positions. Your confidence increases as you perfect your shooting skills, learn to use more weapons, overcome obstacles, and rely on your platoon. In the final weeks, you go through rigorous testing to ensure you are ready for combat as a U.S. Army soldier.[1] This type of military training is similar to what we experience in the body of Christ.

> You therefore must endure hardship as a good soldier of Jesus Christ. No one engaged in warfare entangles himself with the affairs of this life, that he may please him who enlisted him as a soldier.
>
> —2 Timothy 2:3-4

God calls us to be skillful warriors. When you come to Christ, He partners you with the Holy Spirit to take you through spiritual training. First, God builds you up in His Word to renew your mind. The Holy Spirit teaches you how to wield the Word: "For the word of God is living and powerful, and sharper than any two-edged sword, piercing even to the division of soul and spirit..." (Hebrews 4:12). Second Samuel 22:31 says, "As for God, His way is perfect; The word of the Lord is proven; He is a shield to all who trust in Him." A good soldier knows his or her weapons: how they are constructed, the damage they can inflict, and how to use them. To be a good soldier, first you must know the Word of God, which is the most important weapon available to you. Later, you will learn about two more key weapons that you will need to fight.

During your training process as a believer, your stamina and confidence are developed through daily exercise: prayer, study, and meditation on Scripture. Just as in the army, you have to be ready to engage at all times. Throughout military training, soldiers are awakened in the middle of the night and expected to be ready to fight. One of the first things they are conditioned to do is grab their weapon. As a soldier in the army of God, when the Holy Spirit wakes you up at night, get up and grab your Word. Read and seek out what the Lord has to say to you; He may provide you with the intel, instructions, and knowledge you will need to fight.

AUTHORITY IN JESUS CHRIST

Authority means power to influence thought or behavior. An authority can also be referred to as a person who is seen as an expert. In the military, soldiers must follow a chain of command—the hierarchy of authority. Commanding officers provide the limits through which soldiers have the freedom to act. Obeying authority is more than an exercise in following the rules. When authority is ignored, misunderstood, or applied improperly, military actions can be viewed as illegitimate or even criminal.[2]

As believers, when we battle to see the will of God come to pass, we have to know that we fight from a place of authority. All authority has been given to Jesus Christ in heaven and on earth; our authority to war and overcome all of the power of the enemy was given to us by Him (see Matthew 28:18; Luke 10:17-19; 2 Thessalonians 3:3). Your spirit is seated with Him in heaven and you have access to the spirit of wisdom and revelation in Him (see Ephesians 1:17, 2:6). You are an heir of God and a joint-heir with Christ, and you are more than a conqueror through Him who loved you (see Romans 8:16-17, 37). You must not fight under your own name, authority, or strength. That will result in certain defeat. Your authority in Christ makes the following tools available for you to use in the midst of battle:

- *The Blood of Jesus:* Hebrews 10:19 says that through the blood of Jesus, we can boldly enter the Holiest place, where God dwells. With his death, burial, and resurrection, Jesus' blood provided a new and living way for us to come to the Father. We also overcome the enemy by the blood of the Lamb and the word of our testimony (see Revelation 12:11).

- *The Name of Jesus:* When we say the name of Jesus, we wield His power and authority. God has given Christ the name that is above every name, that at the name of Jesus every knee should bow, of those in heaven, and of those on the earth, and of those under the earth, and that every tongue should confess that Jesus Christ is Lord, to the glory of God the Father (see Philippians 2:9-11).

- *The Authority of the Word:* We must know the Word of God to assert its authority. Ephesians 6:17-18 says, "... and the sword of the Spirit, which is the word of God; praying always with all prayer and supplication in the Spirit, being watchful to this end with all perseverance and supplication for all the saints."

- *The Spiritual Position of Jesus:* Christ is seated in heaven, at the right hand of the Father, far above all principality and power and might and dominion, and every name that is named... (see Ephesians 1:20-23). God has highly exalted Him and given Him the name that is above every name.

In warfare, you can plead the blood of Jesus over people, places and things; declare the name of Jesus to establish his sovereignty over all; decree the Word to cause circumstances to align with the will of

God; and glory in the position of Jesus that He is seated in the heavenlies, far above any other power or name.

THE WHOLE ARMOR OF GOD

Military men and women wear uniforms including helmets, padding, and other specially designed gear to protect themselves in the heat of battle. In the body of Christ your spiritual uniform is the whole armor of God. This is a key layer of defense, with offensive elements, that must be in place before you engage in combat.

> Finally, my brethren, be strong in the Lord and in the power of His might. Put on the whole armor of God, that you may be able to stand against the wiles of the devil. For we do not wrestle against flesh and blood, but against principalities, against powers, against the rulers of the darkness of this age, against spiritual hosts of wickedness in the heavenly places. Therefore, take up the whole armor of God, that you may be able to withstand in the evil day, and having done all, to stand.
>
> —Ephesians 6:10-13

I believe the "evil day" in this scripture refers to the opposing forces and entities that you face. Believer, you are not exempt from the enemy. You must confront demonic forces. During your Christian journey you will be challenged in your faith. Opposition and calamity will be loosed against you. This is not a possibility, but a certainty. Nothing in Scripture indicates that as a believer you will avoid these trials. So, you must be prepared to go through them. The Word instructs us to clothe ourselves in the armor of God so that we can stand against the wiles of the devil. Let's look at the first century Roman soldiers to understand the importance of our armor.

- *Belt of Truth:* Also referred to as a "girdle," this was a loose garment tied around the soldier's waist that hung down to their knees, covering the loins. For believers, the belt of truth is the Word of God. If you are not well-versed in Scripture, you will be deceived by the enemy's lies and hindered in deploying your other weapons (see Ephesians 6:14; Psalm 51:6).

- *Breastplate of Righteousness:* This part of the armor protects vital organs, including the heart, and deflects direct attacks. Without it, you may be led by your emotions, which are seated in your heart. The breastplate is not derived from our own righteousness, but that which comes from our faith in Christ (see Proverbs 4:23; 2 Corinthians 6:7; Philippians 3:9 NAS).

- *Shoes of the Gospel of Peace:* These shoes were heavy with spiked soles that helped soldiers to stand firm in battle. They improved mobility, allowing soldiers to march long distances with speed. Soldiers who have feet shod with shoes of peace are able to deliver good news and proclaim salvation (see Ephesians 6:15 and Isaiah 52:7).

- *Shield of Faith:* This weapon is rectangular and covers the length of the body, enabling a soldier to fully protect him or herself during an attack. In the Greek language, shield also means "door" because of its size and shape. By deploying the shield of faith, we protect everything that is valuable to us: ourselves, family, finances, and possessions (see Ephesians 6:16).

- *Helmet of Salvation:* The helmet protects the head and the mind while in the trenches of war. This is important because the mind itself is a battleground (I will share more about this in a moment). Protecting your head keeps you sober-minded. When you are wounded in this area you will lose your effectiveness in battle (see Ephesians 6:17; 1 Thessalonians 5:8; Isaiah 59:17; 1 Peter 1:13).

- *Sword of the Spirit:* The sword of the Spirit—the Word of God—is both defensive and offensive. It is quick and powerful, sharper than a double-edged sword. When you fight, it cuts and penetrates the soul and spirit of your enemy. The devil may attack, but when you speak the Word a sword is formed in the spirit that drives him from your presence (see Ephesians 6:17; Hebrews 4:12; Revelation 1:16).

Before I move on, I want to revisit one piece of your armor—the helmet. Putting on the helmet of salvation is key to taking authority over the battleground of your mind. It is in your mind that you can sabotage yourself through human reasoning, or be attacked by the enemy with negative thinking, vain imaginations, and speculations. Do not allow yourself to be defeated before you even enter the battle. Pray the following scriptures to maintain control over your mind and thoughts:

You will keep him in perfect peace, Whose mind is stayed on You, because he trusts in You.

—Isaiah 26:3

Therefore submit to God. Resist the devil and he will flee from you. Draw near to God and He will draw near to you. Cleanse your hands, you sinners; and purify your hearts, you double-minded.

—James 4:7-8

SECURING THE VICTORY

The final piece to establishing a foundation for spiritual warfare is knowing that you are assured victory. You have already won, and it is only through what Christ has done for you (see 1 John 4:4). He promised to disarm principalities and powers, to make an open spectacle of them, and cause you to triumph (see Colossians 2:15). But, believer, you are still called to war. You are not exempt. Even though the fight is fixed, you have to engage in the battle. God's plan is for you to share in Christ's victory by taking part in it. Matthew 11:12 says, "...the kingdom of heaven suffers violence, and the violent take it by force." The word "force" in the Greek language is *harpazo*, which means to forcibly take possession of, or lay hold to and seize.[3] You must fight violently and eagerly with your full confidence in God. Stand firm in your position in Christ and grab hold of what belongs to you. The beauty is not in you winning the fight. It is in the demonstration and celebration of what has already been won. Jesus, through the shedding of His blood, death on the cross, and resurrection, has shown the whole world that He has defeated Satan's kingdom. Saints, we win, so thank Him in advance!

> The LORD will cause your enemies who rise against you to be defeated before your face; they shall come out against you one way and flee before you seven ways.
>
> —Deuteronomy 28:7

> Now thanks be to God who always leads us in triumph in Christ...
>
> —2 Corinthians 2:14

Chapter 2

WEAPONS OF WAR: PRAYER AND INTERCESSION

It shall come to pass
That before they call, I will answer;
And while they are still speaking, I will hear.

—Isaiah 65:24

'Call to Me, and I will answer you, and show you great and mighty things, which you do not know.'

—Jeremiah 33:3

Therefore I say to you, whatever things you ask when you pray, believe that you receive them, and you will have them.

—Mark 11:24

We have established that in preparing for spiritual warfare, the Word of God is essential. Knowing the Word through study and meditation gives you a solid foundation on which to stand and fight. Now we are ready to discuss the next key weapons in your arsenal: prayer and intercession.

WHAT IS PRAYER?

Prayer is talking to God. It is alerting Him to your needs or the needs of those around you through your own confession. Engaging the Father in this way demonstrates your faith and reliance on Him to bring about change. God is your ultimate back-up and you cannot enter into warfare without first petitioning Him. Consulting God, in Jesus' name, ensures you will receive an answer from Him (see John 14:13, 15:16, 16:23-24). I will further explore answered prayer in a moment.

To pray is to make a fervent request, or a reverent petition to God—to interrogate, call, or invite. It also means an uttered contemplation, wish, or supplication. Prayer is not merely reciting words. It is dialogue between God and His people. Ultimately, prayer is a way for you to connect, commune, and fellowship with the Father. Psalm 65:2 says, "O You who hear prayer, to You all flesh will come." Prayer is alive, energizing, and inspiring. The one who prays revitalizes themselves and the things around them. It is the believer's power source and a conduit to change circumstances in your life and the lives of others. It is vital to use the Word of God in prayer. When you pray according to the Word, He hears you, and you will have what you ask.

> Now this is the confidence that we have in Him, that if we ask anything according to His will, He hears us. And if we know that He hears us, whatever we ask, we know that we have the petitions that we have asked of Him.
>
> —1 John 5:14-15

James 5:16 says, "The effective, fervent prayer of a righteous man avails much." Fervent prayers are intense, passionate, enthusiastic, violent, and fiery. You are the righteousness of God through faith in Christ and your prayers have the capacity to break through anything. You have a right to petition God in prayer, and He has promised to answer. Through answering, God releases revelation and increases your knowledge in the things of Him.

Airplanes and ships use compasses as critical instruments to guide their way and make sure they get to their destinations. Similarly, prayer guides you. It points you in the right direction and tells you where you are going. It alerts you when you are off track and helps you to correct your course. Without prayer, you will roam aimlessly in cycles and patterns that do not bring forth visible fruit. Remember, in prayer God is the navigator. All you have to do is follow his lead. As a believer, you must be committed to pray and know that your prayers are needed to change the world.

Prayer has the capacity to transform nations, but it also transforms you. It is a heart study. It reveals your motives and pinpoints your spiritual position. Prayer exposes your weaknesses, but always directs you to the heavenly Father. In prayer, you subject your soul—your mind, will and emotions—to God. It can be a place of purging because God deals with your iniquity as you come to Him. "To You, O LORD, I lift up my soul," (Psalm 25:1). Prayer stirs and changes you. This is when deliverance can occur. As you submit yourself to God, you give Him permission to get the devil out of you. And over time He is able to draw out your purpose and use you for His glory.

SPIRITUAL LAWS OF ANSWERED PRAYER

The power of prayer is unchanging. It stands when all else fails. You must pray when you have an intense desire to see something come to pass. But to see results takes hard work and consistency. Prayer must be done continuously (see 1 Thessalonians 5:17), because the enemy will do whatever he can to keep you from it. To effectively wield prayer as a weapon and receive answers from the Lord, you must practice the following spiritual laws:

Abide

To abide means to reside in, remain in, comply with, or indwell. Abiding is a two-way exchange: we spend time in God's presence, and He resides in us. Meet God in the secret place by entering your room, shutting the door, and spending time with Him (see Matthew 6:6). When you abide in God, and are in conscious union with Christ, you can ask anything, and it will be done. John 15:7 says, "If you abide in Me, and My words abide in you, you will ask what you desire, and it shall be done for you." The fruit of abiding in Christ is a desire to keep abiding in Him. This gives us the freedom to continuously draw from the fullness of His joy (see Psalm 16:11).

Be Humble

The tallest people in the world are those willing to get on their knees and bow in prayer. This is a posture of humility before the Father. When you are humble, you are meek and modest with an unassuming nature. In humility you are positioned to fight and also to be elevated. "Therefore humble yourselves under the mighty hand of God, that He may exalt you in due time..." (1 Peter 5:6). The battle can only be won on your knees.

Confess

There is power in confessing your wrongs. It unlocks the ability to have continued intimacy with God. First John 1:9 says that if we confess our sins, the Father is faithful and just to forgive our sins and cleanse us of all unrighteousness. In 2 Chronicles 7:14, the Lord says, "...if My people, who are called by My name, will humble themselves, and pray and seek my face, and turn from their wicked ways, then I will hear from heaven, and will forgive their sin and heal their land."

Ask

Asking God involves petitioning Him—going to Him with your concerns and requests. Imagine yourself sitting with God, and talking like you would do in a normal conversation with another person. Luke 11:9 says, "So I say to you, ask, and it will be given to you; seek, and you will find; knock, and it will be opened to you." When you ask in prayer, believe, and you will receive (see Matthew 21:22).

Believe

When you pray, remember that you are coming to the One who created the universe. The god who answers by fire—he is God (see 1 Kings 18:24). He sees and knows all, and has the ability to produce the results you seek. Being double-minded, praying without faith, and wavering weakens your position. It is displeasing to God (see Hebrews 11:6). Hebrews 10:23 says, "Let us hold fast the confession of our hope without wavering, for He who promised is faithful." Ask God to help you in your unbelief and He will (see Mark 9:24).

Agree

There is power in agreeing with another in prayer. With agreement, you must have an assurance of unity in your spirit with the other person(s) so that the matter you are praying about will be established (see Deuteronomy 19:15). Matthew 18:19-20 says, "Again I say to you that if two of you agree on earth concerning anything that they ask, it will be done for them by My Father in heaven. For where two or three are gathered together in My name, I am there in the midst of them."

Persevere

Sometimes you have to trouble God about a matter. In other words, you must be persistent. Don't fall into the trap of thinking that if you pray one time you don't have to pray anymore. In Luke 18:1-8 the widow's relentlessness in prayer caused God to act. Verse seven says, "And shall God not avenge His own elect who cry out day and night to Him, though he bears long with them?" When you lose heart or grow faint and weary, pray. Luke 6:12 says, "Now it came to pass in those days that He went out to the mountain to pray, and continued all night in prayer to God." In the place of prayer, you must endure.

Hindrances to Prayer

To prepare for warfare we must be proactive in building strong and effective prayer lives. There are many distractions that can block us in prayer. Sometimes we hinder ourselves due to our own disobedience and sometimes it is the enemy's doing. Prayer requires obedience, discipline, and the ability to push through. It is important to recognize the traps that will prevent us from praying.

Fear is the number one blockage to effective prayer and is behind most of the hindrances listed here. Second Timothy 1:7 says, "For God has not given us a spirit of fear, but of power and of love and of a sound mind." You cannot fear your enemy because God Himself fights for you (see Deuteronomy 3:22). Even when you are fearful, you must press on in prayer, for God is with you (see Isaiah 41:10; Psalm 56:3).

Another key hindrance to prayer is legalism: the excessive adherence to a law or way of doing things. The devil is usually behind this. He will tell you that to pray effectively, you have to check off a list of religious "do's and don'ts". He will condemn you with legalistic rules, and a record of your iniquities to shame you, bind you, and convince you that God will not hear or answer your prayers. Believer, do not allow your heart to become weighed down by the condemnation of the enemy. He is the accuser of the brethren (see Romans 8:1; 1 John 3:21; Revelation 12:10).

Focusing our attention on the cares of this world, being anxious, and a lack of thanksgiving, also hold us back in prayer (see Matthew 6:34; Philippians 4:6). Some of us are wrapped up in self-pity and harboring unforgiveness (see Mark 11:25-26). This behavior goes directly against what we are called to do as believers. You cannot overlook your sins and thrive in prayer. Before you begin to pray, ask God to expose your iniquity (see Psalm 139:23). Psalm 66:18 says, "If I regard iniquity in my heart, the Lord will not hear." In Proverbs 28:9 we see that, "One who turns away his ear from hearing the law, even his prayer is an abomination." You must take your eyes off of yourself, natural circumstances, or what others may have done to you and focus on the Lord (see Hebrews 12:1-2). Fixing your eyes on Him is doing what is pleasing in his sight. God desires that we live in holiness (see 2 Timothy 2:19-20; 1 Peter 1:15-16). And prayer operates in the lives of those who provide God with clean, righteous vessels (see 1 Peter 3:12).

Knowing and understanding your identity in God is vital in prayer. You can be assured of the effectiveness of your prayers based on your relationship with God and who you are in Him. You are the righteousness of God through faith in Christ Jesus (see Romans 3:22). When you go into prayer, you show up as a son or daughter. That means you don't have to beg God—He's your Father.

You can ask Him anything that is in line with His will, and believe that He hears and will answer you. Have faith that God will make good on his promises. Do not doubt, but believe that whatsoever you ask in His name, you will receive (see John 14:13-14). Isaiah 55:11 says, "So shall My word be that goes forth from My mouth; it shall not return to Me void, but it shall accomplish what I please, and it shall prosper in the thing for which I sent it." You do not need a special credential, title, or position to pray. You do not need a certain skill or intelligent words. You are authorized by the blood of Jesus. He is all you need.

You cannot maintain an effective prayer life and entertain the devil's lies. You have to choose one or the other. James 4:7 says, "Therefore submit to God. Resist the devil and he will flee from you." Make the decision that you are going to pray no matter what is going on around you. God is waiting to hear from you. He is ready to give you revelation, wisdom and the answers to your problems. Remember, a prayer that is never prayed cannot be answered.

Battling in Prayer

Now that we have addressed how to position yourself to receive answers to prayer, let's talk about execution. This is where the battle truly begins.

Prayer is embarking upon the supernatural—the unseen realm. While we may initiate prayer by using the Word of God, one of the most powerful ways for us to pray is in the Spirit. When you pray in the Spirit, using your heavenly language, you are praying the perfect will of God with the Holy Spirit's help. The Holy Spirit knows the things of God: "For what man knows the things of a man except the spirit of the man which is in him? Even so no one knows the things of God except the Spirit of God," (see 1 Corinthians 2:11). It is by the Holy Spirit that you receive everything that you need to be successful in battle, including instruction, wisdom, and foresight. When you don't know how to pray, you can rely on the Holy Spirit. Romans 8:26a says, "Likewise the Spirit also helps in our weaknesses. For we do not know what we should pray for as we ought..." When you pray in the Spirit the mysteries of God are unveiled. The Holy Spirit ensures that you not only receive spiritual intel, but also the strategic insight that you need to fight with precision.

When we pray, we violently shake the heavens. We are pulling down strongholds to see the Father's will manifest in the earth. To cut you off from the promises of God, the enemy erects stone-like barriers that seem impenetrable. These stone walls can be torn down, but only by the earnest use of a hammer. That's what prayer becomes when you use the Word of God and your heavenly language. It breaks down the hard places. Jeremiah 23:29 says, "Is not My word like a fire?" says the LORD, "And like a hammer that breaks the rock in pieces?" The key is that you must use God's hammer with diligence. That means you have to keep hitting those difficult, unyielding places in prayer. And you cannot stop praying until you have broken through. You must pray nonstop until God has assured you of victory.

Praying with others, or corporately, increases the impact of prayer (see Acts 4:31, 12:5-17; Matthew 18:19). Everyone you pray with does not have to be at the same level of spiritual maturity for your prayers to be powerful. It's the combination of consistency, strategy, and tactics based on the Word of God that brings breakthrough. Consistent prayer releases cumulative power. This is why we always have to pray. Our prayers accumulate and build strength to bring light to dark places.

You must keep praying, whether you see what you desire come to pass or not. When wielded properly, prayer is a force to be reckoned with. It is a weapon of mass destruction that can penetrate any realm, nation, city, or person. It demolishes the walls of the enemy like a battering ram (see Ezekiel 21:22, 26:9). But to be effective, prayer must be deployed. Saints, let us pray!

INTERCESSION

So I sought for a man among them who would make a wall, and stand in the gap before Me on behalf of the land, that I should not destroy it; but I found no one.

—Ezekiel 22:30

> He saw that there was no man, and wondered that
> there was no intercessor; therefore His own arm
> brought salvation for Him; and His own righteous-
> ness, it sustained Him.
>
> —Isaiah 59:16

WHAT IS INTERCESSION?

In spiritual warfare, intercession is the companion to prayer. We have established that prayer is dialoguing with God; it is communion and fellowship with Him. Prayer is directed towards God. Intercession, however, is working with God. It is standing in the gap for people and situations. Intercession builds on the concept of prayer, but moves beyond personal conversation with God about our own thoughts, desires, and needs. It opens the way for us to approach God with the needs of other people, even other nations.[1]

Intercession is negotiating for or against something—crying out to God for His intervention. It also means to entreat and rush against opposing forces with the intent of overthrowing. Other terms for intercession include going in between, pleading for another, and representing one party to another. For the ultimate model of intercession, we can look to our Lord and Savior, Jesus Christ.

As our chief intercessor, Jesus stood between God and humanity to reconcile us to the Father. 1 Timothy 2:5 says, "For there is one God and one Mediator between God and men, the Man Christ Jesus..." By fulfilling his role as mediator, Jesus broke Satan's hold off of mankind. He was empowered by the Holy Spirit, and He has given us the Spirit to help us as we intercede. "Now He who searches the hearts knows what the mind of the spirit is, because He makes intercession for the saints according to the will of God," (Romans 8:27). Our role in intercession is to be an extension of the work that Jesus did. And our intercessory call is to release God's power, authority, and dominion—to stand in the gap, and enforce His will in the earth.

Intercession, through intense battle, is a means for Christ to be formed in the saints. The Apostle Paul said, "My little children, of whom I travail in birth again until Christ be formed in you," (Galatians 4:19 KJV). To travail means to labor, toil, or struggle. It is hard work.

We can view travailing in intercession much like a wrestling match. In Genesis 32:24-28 we see that Jacob wrestled with God all night and refused to let Him go until he was blessed. He would not relent. God touched the socket of his right thigh, and Jacob emerged from the match a changed man. Not only did he receive the blessing he labored for, but he also had a limp and a new name. When we intercede, we get into the face of God. The place where Jacob wrestled with God is called *Penuel*, also spelled Peniel, which means "face of God" in Hebrew.[2] When he came face to face with God, Jacob was in a place of brokenness and desperation. He thought his brother Esau was going to kill him because he'd stolen his birthright and their father's blessing. He was determined to come away from the encounter with everything he needed from the Lord.

Intercession can lead to significant changes in your life, as we see with Jacob. Sometimes you feel weary, discouraged, or defeated in intercession, but you must resolve to fight on. The result could not only be an answer to the matter you have before the Father, but also fresh revelation, a light for your path, or transformation in an area of your life. When you pray and intercede you have to hold fast to your confidence and rejoice in hope firmly to the end (see Hebrews 3:6).

In intercession, you conquer your opponent—the enemy—by applying unrelenting pressure. Just as the devil imposes heaviness and burdens on God's people, you as a saint have to shift the weight back onto him. And you have to battle until you get a release. In the midst, you learn how to work with the Lord and how to stand in the gap for your nation, city, family, and friends. Faith is essential to successful spiritual warfare. And you will have victory by releasing your faith in the Lord (see Proverbs 21:31 NAS). In the end, you will know that you have neutralized the enemy and won the battle when you receive a witness—an agreement—through the Holy Spirit (see Romans 8:31; Psalm 44:5).

WHY INTERCEDE?

God calls us to intercede for two important reasons: to represent Him, and serve as watchmen over the affairs of the earth. Just as with prayer, believers must be aware of the key hindrances that may hold them back in intercession. To overcome these potential blocks, you must understand your role in the earth, the commitment to pressing through adversity, and how to hit your target with precision.

In the Father's Image

Prayer and intercession are ways for mankind to reflect God in the earth. God created people in His image, as a shadow or an illusion of Himself. In Hebrew, the word *tselem*, means similar or comparable to God.[3] Our connection to God should show people a picture of what and who He is. This does not mean that you are a god, but that you have His attributes. Psalm 8:5-6 says, "For You have made him a little lower than the angels, and You have crowned him with glory and honor. You have made him to have dominion over the works of Your hands; You have put all things under his feet..." Being crowned with glory means you carry a heavy weight of authority in the spirit realm. Your position in the kingdom is to dominate. All things, including the enemy, are under your feet.

As you pray and intercede, you engage heaven to move on your behalf. When you intercede, it releases God to bring redemption, salvation, and healing to all man-kind. The Greek word *mishael* means one who God chose to govern over the earth.[4] God gave every one of us the responsibility to govern. Psalm 115:16 says, "The heaven, even the heavens, are the LORD's; but the earth He has given to the children of men." God has given us the earth to oversee and mediate so that, through us, He can work out His divine plans. In God's likeness, and through our weapons of prayer and intercession, we become a pow-erful force to engage in warfare, and reign in the earth.

Watchmen, Lift Your Voices

Intercessors are called to be watchmen. God can't accom-plish His will in the earth if He can't find an intercessor to labor alongside Him (see Isaiah 59:16; Ezekiel 22:30). The world is a mess, and it is not because of governmental leaders or civil disobedience. It is because intercessors are not fulfilling their role in the earth. Intercessors must lock arms with God and be willing to wrestle with Him in deep prayer, as Jacob did. By doing this, they become a bridge for people to cross over and help to maintain God's hedge of protection around them. Daniel persevered in prayer and intercession (see Daniel 9, 10). He stayed on his knees in worship and confessed his sins, and that of the people, Israel. In a vision, a messenger told Daniel that the king of Persia withstood him for twenty-one days, until the archangel Michael came to help. In other words, God's response was delayed because of interference from the enemy. Daniel understood intercession and he committed himself to persevering in it—even pushing through unknown battles in the heavenlies. As a result, God heard Daniel's prayer and answered him.

Hindrances to Intercession

Not understanding the truth about humanity's role in governing the earth is a key hindrance in intercession. Since God is sovereign, you may wonder why you need to pray and intercede. The answer is found in Genesis 1:26-27, where He gives Adam and Eve dominion over the earth. God does not go against His Word. He cannot move unless you do.

The Bible says that we ought to pray according to Mark 11:24-25, scriptures that we have referenced previously. Just as with prayer, in intercession we often stop short of seeing a breakthrough because we lack endurance. This is one of the greatest causes of defeat in intercession. We do not wait well. We live in a society of convenience, where we receive things immediately. We are accustomed to formulas—following a certain path and seeing results right away. And we place that same expectation on God. Many intercessors today are fatigued and spiritually bankrupt because they expect God to show up in an instant. The truth is, we are not automatically granted answers to prayer or results in intercession. We have to labor and push through to see the changes that need to come forth.

Not fasting regularly also can hinder intercession. Sometimes we need to fast to prepare ourselves to intercede, so that our minds and hearts are clear, and we have the energy we need to engage with the Lord. Also, you may feel as if you don't know how to intercede effectively. Remember, the Holy Spirit is your helper and praying in the Spirit is powerful. In intercession, the Holy Spirit will help you to be precise by praying God's perfect will through you, to ensure you hit your target. You must aim to strike the mark and not be one who beats the air (see 1 Corinthians 9:26). The word "strike" is translated in Hebrew as *paga*, meaning to entreat, attack, and encounter with hostility or violence.[5] It means to meet together, intercede, or reach. To achieve success in intercession, you have to keep hitting or striking a specific target (see Numbers 35:19; 2 Samuel 1:15).

Prayer and intercession function differently, but are complementary. These weapons must be used together for effective warfare. Combined with your foundation of the Word of God and the empowerment of the Holy Spirit—these are the first weapons that you will rely on as you prepare to war in the spirit realm.

Chapter 3

CONFIGURING YOUR WEAPONS

For though we walk in the flesh, we do not war according to the flesh. For the weapons of our warfare are not carnal but mighty in God for pulling down strongholds, casting down arguments and every high thing that exalts itself against the knowledge of God, bringing every thought into captivity to the obedience of Christ.

—2 Corinthians 10:3-5

You have learned how to train for warfare through knowledge and understanding of the Word of God and the power of the Holy Spirit. And you should now be familiar with prayer and intercession—your weapons of war. Now it is time to learn how to configure these weapons to intensify your attacks against the enemy's camp.

In the first chapter I mentioned that in military boot camp, soldiers are trained to engage in battle with an M16A2 rifle. While it's a standard-issued weapon, it is sophisticated, versatile, and multi-functional in nature. It can be positioned at the shoulder or hip, and discharge ammunition with automatic (three-round bursts) or semiautomatic (single shot) fire. It has a fully adjustable rear sight, an optical device that allows for accurate aim, and a compensator which helps keep the muzzle down during firing.[1] These rifles are complex, and have many other features that affect their weight, impact how they function with different types of gear, and increase their range when firing.[2]

In the spirit, the precision of your prayers and intercession can be intensified with specific principles, actions, vocabulary, and even angelic assistance. When used strategically, these tools open up God's counsel and insight to believers. As a result, your weapons can be used effectively to confuse and disrupt the enemy's camp. Ultimately, by enhancing your weapons with the following principles, you will be able to neutralize Satan's power and plans.

Spiritual Principles in Action

- *Faith:* Engaging in spiritual warfare must begin from a place of taking God at His Word. Have faith in Him and believe that through the power and authority He has given you, nothing is impossible (see Mark 11:22-23).

- *Fasting:* Denying your flesh is vital to hearing clearly from the Lord. By abstaining from food, entirely or in part, you can intentionally seek God's instructions for how to break yokes and release burdens (see Isaiah 58:6; Matthew 6:17).

- *The Anointing:* God's oil of anointing destroys yokes. Through the Spirit of the Lord, we are anointed to bring healing and freedom to the people and places that are in need (see Isaiah 10:27; Luke 4:18).

- *Boldness:* It is God's will that you enter warfare with the spirit of boldness. This is His way of terrorizing the enemy. With boldness in prayer and intercession, you can overcome your own fear, intimidation, and insecurity (see 2 Timothy 1:7; Hebrews 10:19).

- *Marching/Stomping/Clapping/Dancing:* God directs us to use what we have to war against the enemy—our feet, hands, and the movement of our bodies. In peace, He promises to crush the devil under your feet, and that marching for an appointed time will bring victory. Praise including clapping and dancing can weaken the enemy's line of defense and allow you to overcome (see Romans 16:20; Joshua 6:2-17; Psalm 47:1).

- *Shouting:* Your voice is another powerful weapon to use against the enemy. You can declare the Word of God through shouting and singing loudly with boldness. You are called to praise the Lord in all of His holiness (see Psalm 47:1b; 2 Chronicles 20:22; Joshua 6:20).

- *Silence:* Using wisdom, there are times when you are called to be silent. The Father often communicates to us with a still, small voice. To hear Him clearly, we have to be quiet. For Elijah, this action led to him putting on his mantle to prophesy for the Lord (see 1 Kings 19:11-13).

- *Contending:* When you contend, you dispute, battle, fight, struggle, and argue in the spirit realm to manifest victory in the earth. Contending requires consistent and vigorous engagement with your enemy. Arm yourself for war and go to battle against the Midianites—those who would cause strife (see Numbers 31:3-4).

- *Rebuking:* This means to reprove sharply, admonish or reprimand. It is a strong and authoritative expression of disapproval. The Lord rebukes the enemy and we can assert this truth against him (see Jude 1:9; Isaiah 1:17; Proverbs 1:23).

WARFARE LANGUAGE

- *Pulling Down Strongholds:* Strongholds are defined as fortified cities. These are territories or places that the enemy has taken hold of in people's lives. Pulling down the walls of these cities can be challenging, but it is possible with God at your side (see 2 Kings 11:8).

- *Establishing Divine Parameters and Boundaries:* Confirming God's boundaries for your battle will ensure that your foot will not slip and that you are well-able to overcome and destroy your enemy (see 2 Samuel 22:37-41).

- *Dispossessing:* This means to put out of occupancy or possession. In prayer, we can dispossess territorial spirits that block progress, blessings, and answers to prayer. The prince of Persia is the territorial spirit referenced in the book of Daniel, that held up the messenger sent to Daniel. The warring angel Michael was sent to release the messenger to fulfill his assignment (see Daniel 9:20-24, 10:13).

- *Binding and Loosing:* Binding is an exercise by which we immobilize the enemy. This means the enemy is bound and unable to move or carry out his plan. We must bind the strongman that Satan has placed in various structures and entities

in the earth, and we must loose the spirit
of God in the land or the fruit of the Spirit in people's lives (see Matthew 12:29,
16:19, 18:18; Galatians 5:22-23).

ANGELIC ASSISTANCE

Psalm 91:11 says that God gives his angels charge over us, to keep us in all of our ways. The word "charge" means to appoint a messenger; meaning, the angels not only assist us, but they watch over us as well. 2 Samuel 14:20 says that David is as wise as an angel. Wise means shrewd, cunning, prudent, and clever. Many believers are unclear about the role of angels because there is little teaching or incorrect doctrine about them. Angels are like our heavenly platoon. They are our back up in the spirit, poised and ready to assist us at all times. We saw in Exodus 14 that the Lord contends for us, but He also has provided angels to help us as we war. Angels are positioned with God in heaven, and just as in the military, they hold various degrees of station and rank.

Psalm 8:5a says that Jesus was made a little lower than the angels, which means the same applies to us. However, we do not worship angels. And while angels are designated to help us, the Holy Spirit is our number one source for guidance, direction, and help. Angels are sent forth by God as ministering spirits to support heirs of salvation. Heirs of salvation are those who have received Jesus Christ as their Lord and Savior (see Hebrews 1:14). God, in His wisdom and power, has released angels to aid us in achieving our destiny and purpose. Angels have intelligence and wisdom and we can ask God for their assistance in battle. Later, I will share an example of how I enlisted angels to help me during spiritual warfare, and the breakthrough that came as a result.

As we saw earlier in the section on intercession, when Daniel prayed we know he was heard because angels were dispatched. The same happens when we pray. Remember in Daniel 10, the messenger who had the answer to Daniel's prayer tried to get to him but was delayed because he was held by Satan's evil angel. Michael the archangel was dispatched to fight in the heavenlies. His intervention made sure that the message from the Lord and answer to prayer got to Daniel. Later in Daniel 12:1, we see that Michael had the responsibility to guard over the people of God and his purposes.

In warfare, you can ask God to release His angels that excel in strength and heed the voice of the Lord, and along with all His hosts, fight to do His pleasure in all places of His dominion (see Psalm 103:20-22). Ask God to release Michael to fight against the Persian empires and those holding you and others in bondage. When you pray, have confidence that you are setting things in motion in the heavenlies. God is releasing angels against Satan's opposition to your answered prayer. He needs your help to fulfill His mission and He has provided you reinforcement through the ministry of angels.

Chapter 4

KNOWING YOUR ENEMY

And the LORD spoke to Moses, saying, 'Send men to spy out the land of Canaan, which I am giving to the children of Israel; from each tribe of their fathers you shall send a man, every one a leader among them..." Then Moses sent them to spy out the land of Canaan, and said to them, "Go up this way into the South, and go up to the mountains, and see what the land is like: whether the people who dwell in it are strong or weak, few or many; whether the land they dwell in is good or bad; whether the cities they inhabit are like camps or strongholds; whether the land is rich or poor; and whether there are forests there or not. Be of good courage. And bring some of the fruit of the land." Now the time was the season of the first ripe grapes.

—Numbers 13:1-2, 17-20

> The thief does not come except to steal, and to kill,
> and to destroy. I have come that they may have life,
> and that they may have it more abundantly.
>
> —John 10:10

In Numbers, before the children of Israel entered into the promised land, the Lord instructed Moses to send men into the land to spy it out. Moses told them to investigate the people who dwelled in the land, assess the quality of the land itself, and determine whether the land was rich or poor. All of this information was designed to help them build a strategy to overtake their enemies so that they could take possession of what God had promised them. By taking a similar approach, we can develop an effective strategy that sets us up for the win.

Before engaging in spiritual warfare, we must take time to study and know the devil. He is a real enemy that we cannot see, who manifests his behavior through people. He accuses us and comes to steal, kill, and destroy. So, we must prepare offensively. We can look at Job 1 and 2 to see the destruction that the enemy causes, even for those who are faithful. "Now there was a day when the sons of God came to present themselves before the LORD, and Satan also came among them. And the LORD said to Satan, 'From where do you come?' So Satan answered the LORD and said, 'From going to and fro on the earth, and from walking back and forth on it,'" (Job 1:6-7). God is aware of Satan and is having a conversation with him about afflicting Job (see Job 1:8-12). Satan first attacks Job's character and then his health. His objective is to make Job lament and feel guilty. It is the same with us. As long as the enemy can make us feel condemned, we cannot defeat him. Guilt is one of the keys to defeat us, but righteousness is the key to victory. Through the cross, God has dealt with all guilt. He has forgiven us for all of our sins (see Colossians 2:14 NIV). Some believers think that because of God's hedge of protection, they are exempt from demonic attacks. Job's story proves that this is not the case. Ecclesiastes 10:8 KJV says that when the hedge of protection is breached, the serpent bites.

This does not mean that we give all credit to the enemy for causing those issues that concern us, but we must be aware of the traps that can form if we choose to not believe in him at all. Believing that Satan does not exist is dangerous and can create pitfalls for followers of Jesus. Second Corinthians 2:11 says that we should not be ignorant of Satan's devices. A device is a trick, cunning plan, or scheme to deceive (see Psalm 21:11, 26:10). Demonic devices are designed to derail believers. As we addressed in our foundations section, the devil's battleground is the mind. If we are not careful, what may begin as simply disregarding the enemy can create a stronghold of unbelief.

SATAN IN ALL HIS FORMS

Satan is known as the devil and Lucifer, which is translated as Day Star or bearer of light (see Matthew 4:1; Isaiah 14:12; Revelation 22:16). Other names for him include the son of perdition, the father of lies, the deceiver of the whole world, the tempter, the ruler of this world, and the prince of the power of the air (see 2 Thessalonians 2:3; John 8:44; Revelation 12:9; Matthew 4:3; John 14:30; Ephesians 2:2). He also is called the angel-prince, or Abaddon, the destroyer or angel of the bottomless pit (see Revelation 9:11). Revelation 12:3-4 depicts him as a great red dragon.

Lucifer was a cherub, who was appointed to lead the heavenly worship assembly into the glory of God's presence. Cherubim are described as winged figures that usually stand in a special nearness to God. They are engaged in the highest adoration and service and always move in accordance with His will (see Psalm 18:10; Ezekiel 10:20; Revelation 4:1-11).[1] Lucifer was known as the anointed cherub. Of all of the Lord's creatures, this designation is given only to him (see Ezekiel 28:14). We can conclude that because of his gifts, he became jealous, full of pride, rebellious, and thought that he should be like God (see Ezekiel 28:1-12). Eventually, he launched an all-out assault on the other angels signaling his decision to enter into an eternal war against the Creator, Almighty God.

Lucifer became the root of all evil in the universe. The Bible says that he was perfect in all of his ways until iniquity was found in him (see Ezekiel 28:15). He boldly attempted to exalt himself above the Master, waging a battle against the mighty throne of God. Because of Lucifer's preeminence and prestige in heaven, he was able to influence lesser angels to rebel against God, drawing them into partnership with him. Ultimately, Lucifer recruited one-third of the angels to join him in executing his plan. They all were cast out of heaven, losing their habitation and divine nature (see Luke 10:18; Revelation 12:7-9). In response to his exile, the book of Revelation says the devil persecuted the woman who brought forth the male Child. He was in opposition with the woman and wanted to make war with the remnant of her seed, who keep the commandments of God and have the testimony of Jesus Christ. Today, this is why the devil attacks mankind and believers in the earth (see Revelation 12:13-17).

Lucifer's Sealed Fate

In Isaiah 14:12-14, Satan made five statements in his heart that demonstrated his intention to battle against the throne of God and confirmed his place in hell.

- *"I will ascend into heaven..."* Having influence in heaven was not enough for Lucifer. He wanted greater and more, and was determined to ascend above the throne of God to overthrow Him. He rebelled against the Father, was exiled to earth, and is destined for hell.

- *"I will exalt my throne above the stars of God..."* God had already given Lucifer great authority. Isaiah 14:13 says that Lucifer envisioned himself being in charge of others, competing, and planning a revolt against God's authority.

- *"I will also sit on the mount of the congregation on the farthest sides of the north..."* Lucifer thought the angels were to assemble on this mountain—Mount Casius in Northern Syria—where witchcraft and the worship of false gods are currently practiced today.

- *"I will ascend above the heights of the clouds..."* Lucifer's pride and arrogance did not falter. He knew no bounds. He truly envisioned himself holding a position higher than that of God.

- *"I will be like the Most High."* Lucifer, in his greatest thirst for power, said he would be like the Almighty God, with equal rule and seniority. With these words he showed covetousness, which is the excessive desire of the possessions of God.

DEMONOLOGY

Satan is the enemy of our souls. He is the one with whom we regularly contend, and the biggest threat to our freedom and ability to fulfill our purpose. We have established that we should never focus solely on him. But, knowing and understanding how he operates, and how this connects to spiritual warfare, is vital. Satan primarily operates through demons. A demon is a disembodied spirit, which means it exists outside of a body; however, it needs a body to operate. Demonology is the study or belief in demons. In the sight of God, demons are evil and unclean. Satan manifests his behavior through people. This happens when he gains access to their souls through open doors such as sin, generational issues, or curses decreed against them. This is why most people, organizations, and countries operate under some level of dysfunction. And this is why people need deliverance—the act of casting out demonic spirits. Teaching about demons is largely ignored in the church today. Yet, healing and deliverance are key to defeating Satan, sin, and death.

Battling in the Heavenlies

The heavens are filled with the principalities of evil. The term "heavens" refers to one of three realms. Hebrews 4:14 says, "Seeing then that we have a great High Priest who has passed through the heavens, Jesus the Son of God..." Additionally, Paul says that he knew a man in Christ who, either in or out of the body, was caught up to the third heaven (see 2 Corinthians 12:2). If there is a third heaven, there must be a first and a second. Here is a description of all three:

- *The First Heaven:* This includes our immediate atmosphere, about 20 miles above earth. This includes the air that we breathe and the space immediately surrounding the earth. The word translated "air" is *ouranos*, the same Greek word that in other sections of the Bible is translated "heaven," (see Genesis 6:7; James 5:18).

- *The Second Heaven:* Outer space, including the sun, moon and stars, is the celestial, or second heaven. The Bible refers to the stars in heaven as the "heaven of heavens," (see Matthew 24:29; Deuteronomy 4:19, 10:14; Psalm 148:4).

- *The Third Heaven:* God cannot be contained in any one geographical place, yet the third heaven is referred to as the home of God (see 1 Kings 8:27; Hebrews 8:1, 9:24; Acts 7:55; Revelation 4:1-4).[2]

Spiritual warfare, or battling in the spirit realm, takes place in the heavens. Demonic realms include the first and second heavens, which are controlled by principalities. These are ruling spirits that have oversight of regions and territories, and the groups of demons assigned to specific cities, institutions, and even people. Principalities and demonic oppression take hold through openings—also called airways, vortexes, doors, or portals that give them access to people and places. The enemy is only given the right to access people through sinful behavior. This includes thoughts, beliefs, and behaviors that go against the will of God.

While you have been given power over all the power of the enemy, to trample over deadly creatures and not be harmed, you must prepare to fight. He is a defeated foe, but he is extremely skilled at what he does, as he has been using the same strategies and tactics since the beginning of time. Study, know, and understand how he operates, so that in every battle you are assured victory.

Chapter 5

PREPARING FOR BATTLE

Though an army may encamp against me,
My heart shall not fear;
Though war may rise against me,
In this I will be confident.

—Psalm 27:3

In the military, strategy and tactics dictate how warfare is conducted. Strategy involves the careful planning, coordination, and general direction of military operations to meet objectives. It is the overall game plan used to direct the steps and actions of soldiers. Tactics are used to execute the strategy. They are specific, short-term decisions involving the movement of troops and deployment of weapons on the battlefield.[1]

As a believer, and soldier in the army of God, you now should have the knowledge and understanding of all of the tools that you need to engage in spiritual warfare with strength and confidence. You have learned how to:

- Establish a solid foundation in the Word of God, with the empowerment of the Holy Spirit and the authority of Jesus Christ.
- Identify, understand, and use prayer and intercession as your weapons of war.
- Understand and use spiritual principles, vocabulary, and angelic assistance to configure your weapons.
- Know your enemy, Satan, and his strategies.

Now we will focus on pulling together everything you have learned to prepare for war. We will start with some practical points to help keep you in a posture of continuous preparation for the battles that you will face. I encourage you to spend time in prayer and meditation and rely on the Holy Spirit's help in executing these activities in your day-to-day life.

- *Spend time in God's presence* (Psalm 16:11)
- *Read and study the Bible* (Joshua 1:8)
- *Cultivate an atmosphere to hear and receive instruction from God* (2 Peter 1:18)
- *Worship God* (John 4:24)
- *Commit to a life of purity and regularly pray for spiritual cleansing* (Psalm 51:10; 1 John 5:18)
- *Ask God to reveal sin issues* (Psalm 66:18)
- *Pursue pure motives* (Matthew 5:8; Joshua 7:1-9)
- *Maintain a servant's heart* (Mark 9:35; Galatians 5:13; 1 Peter 4:10-11)
- *Guard your heart against jealousy and envy* (Proverbs 4:23)
- *Be at peace with everyone and live in holiness* (Hebrews 12:14)
- *Be humble* (1 Peter 5:6)

Engage the Holy Spirit

As you prepare, the most important thing to remember is that your battle strategy, including how you use your weaponry and knowledge of the enemy to wage war, must be completely guided by the Holy Spirit. This is essential. You can never know exactly how the Lord is going to instruct you to move. His directions are always precise and tailored to each situation. There is no formula and a one-size fits all approach will not work. You will only succeed by following specific instructions from the Lord. The flow and clarity of the directions He gives you will greatly depend on how much time you spend in the Word and in His presence.

Once you have your instructions, the next step is to check your uniform—the armor of God. Tighten your helmet strap, secure your boot laces, ensure your gear is intact, and ready your weapons. Remember the authority that you have been given through Jesus Christ. Lastly, have faith and confidence in God that you will be victorious!

REAL-LIFE EXPERIENCES

I think it is important to share with you some examples of how all of the training, weaponry, and preparation outlined in this book have been effective for me personally as I've ministered around the world. What I have shared with you thus far is based on revelation that I have received from the Lord over many years. In each of the following cases, I sought the Lord for instruction as I prepared to minister. There were some instances when He provided me and our team with intelligence in advance, and sometimes I received revelation right in the midst of ministering. The key for me has always been to prepare with prayer, be sensitive to the voice of the Holy Spirit, be obedient in doing exactly what He instructs, and use my knowledge of the Word to hit the target.

A Miraculous Healing

I was in prayer, preparing to minister that evening with my team. Coming out of my prayer time, the Holy Spirit revealed to me that a spirit of infirmity would be in our midst, and that the power to heal would be present. He gave me Luke 5:17, which says, "One day Jesus was teaching, and Pharisees and teachers of the law were sitting there. They had come from every village of Galilee and from Judea and Jerusalem. And the power of the Lord was with Jesus to heal the sick." I have learned that whenever God wants to do something, He reveals it in the Word. The Word says to quench not the Holy Spirit, so we have to be sure to yield to Him (see 1 Thessalonians 5:19).

God said that He wanted someone to be healed that night. After we began the service, I told the attendees that there were some people present who needed healing. A woman who was part of our ministry came to the altar. She had a cancerous lump in her neck, and her doctors told her that if they removed it, she could lose her ability to speak. This woman happened to sing at our ministry, and the lump was visibly noticeable. I began to pray in the Holy Spirit and said:

"I command angelic assistance to aid this woman now, in the name of Jesus, and the power of God to be released. I release the fire of God to burn up the growth now and call on Jehovah-Rapha—the Lord who heals—in Jesus' name," (see Matthew 14:14; Exodus 15:26).

We watched the knot completely dissolve and disappear from the woman's neck. God healed her instantly. Several members of my team passed out, having never seen a miraculous healing.

Deliverance in Virginia

I was asked to conduct deliverance as part of prophetic and apostolic training for a pastor and her ministry leaders. In preparation for the session, my team and I prayed and asked God to reveal to us the strongholds and any demonic entities that were in the region. The Holy Spirit let us know that there was strong witchcraft being practiced in the area. Specifically, the Lord said that the region was dry. He said there was no water and the people were thirsty for deliverance. God showed us that high-level witchcraft, familiar spirits, and demonic altars were causing the problems. Before ministering, I decreed Leviticus 20:27 NKJV over the region. It says, "A man or a woman who is a medium, or who has familiar spirits, shall surely be put to death; they shall stone them with stones. Their blood shall be upon them." I commanded heaven to release stones, bound up familiar spirits, and asked God to be a consuming fire to release fire upon the demonic altars. I declared Hebrews 10:29: "Of how much worse punishment, do you suppose, will he be thought worthy who has trampled the Son of God underfoot, counted the blood of the covenant by which he was sanctified a common thing, and insulted the Spirit of grace?"

The session was scheduled to be conducted during the day; however, upon arriving, my team and I remarked at how the sky was overcast and dark. The atmosphere felt heavy, as if something was weighing down the area in the spirit. As the Holy Spirit had forewarned us, the church was located in the same vicinity where witchcraft was prevalent. Down the street there were even storefronts for psychics and tarot card readers. As we approached the church, we noticed a number of black birds that looked like crows nesting in trees adjacent to the building. I knew immediately by the Holy Spirit that the birds were on assignment to conduct demonic surveillance. They were there to watch and see what we were doing there. I believe some of the witches in the area actually took the form of these birds to interfere with the deliverance.

Once we were onsite with our hosts, my first objective was to prevent witchcraft from interfering with our activities, so I decreed the following: "I release the sword and the arrows of the Lord to cut the legs of these spirit birds from underneath them and knock them to the ground. I release ministering angels to assist us as we minister to this team," (see Genesis 15:11 ; Job 5:12-14). The birds began to screech. Some fell to the ground and the rest flew away. After we entered the church and began to perform deliverance on our host team, several of them manifested, which was evidence of demonic oppression in the area. Eventually, by that evening the entire team was set free.

Principalities at the U.S.-Canadian Border
In Michigan, near the Canadian border, a ministry was experiencing an unusual number of accidents and premature deaths. The ministry leaders there told me this stemmed from people practicing soothsaying (fortune-telling) and necromancy (worshipping the dead). People were releasing spells in the region as part of their demonic activity. My team was asked to minister in the area to disrupt these attacks by the enemy. In prayer, I asked God for the his-

tory of the region and why the situation existed. The Holy Spirit revealed that the principalities (the ruling spirits) over the region were soothsaying and murder.

After learning this information, my first step was to pray and engage God. I let Him know that we needed to come against soothsaying and murder and began to pray that His will be done on earth as it is in heaven (see Matthew 6:9-13; Hebrews 7:26; Romans 8:26). I asked God for instructions and direction. He advised me to start by praying in tongues and to intercede for the region, city, and people. He said that next I would need to come against witchcraft and another principality—the anti-Christ spirit. My team and I began to war through prayer and intercession, using scriptures that specifically targeted these principalities and the destruction that was resulting from their activity. Over the course of several days, the Holy Spirit began to bear witness with us that the demonic grip over the territory was weakening. We began to do deliverance with individual ministry members. After our time there, we received a testimony from the leaders that accidents were no longer taking place, and people were experiencing freedom.

The purpose for sharing these real-life scenarios is to help you see how the revelation that I have shared with you in this book truly does work. From these examples, you can see how much my team and I relied on prayer, hearing from the Holy Spirit, and the Word of God. Know that some of your battles will end quickly, while others may take longer. Be encouraged, and do not grow weary in the battle (see Galatians 6:9). Stay engaged until the victory comes—no matter how long it takes (see Revelation 20:1-3). Victory is yours!

Chapter 6

WARFARE PRAYERS AND DECREES

Job 22:28 says to decree a thing and it shall be established. To decree is to dictate, ordain, or prescribe. It is to determine or order judicially. This means by law, whatever you say in alignment with the Word of God will be done. When engaging in spiritual warfare, decrees are used for two reasons: 1. To edify and encourage yourself in the Lord; to remind you of with and form whom you battle, and 2. To remind the Lord of what He promised would come to pass (see Psalm 55:11). As you build up your experience and strength in spiritual warfare, you will create your own decrees and prayers using the Word of God. To help you launch into war, here are some foundational decrees to use:

Declaring Your Authority as the Righteous
We have established that you have authority through Christ Jesus. Remind yourself and the enemy of that truth.

Decree:

> "All the horns of the wicked I will also cut off,
> But the horns of the righteous shall be exalted."
>
> —Psalm 75:10

Wisdom, Revelation, and Knowledge
Pray that the spirit of wisdom, revelation, and knowledge be loosed as God, your stronghold brings stability in this time.

Decree:

> I… do not cease to give thanks for you, making mention of you in my prayers: that the God of our Lord Jesus Christ, the Father of glory, may give to you the spirit of wisdom and revelation in the knowledge

of Him, the eyes of your understanding being en-
lightened; that you may know what is the hope of
His calling, what are the riches of the glory of His
inheritance in the saints, and what is the exceeding
greatness of His power toward us who believe, according to the working of His mighty power which
He worked in Christ when He raised Him from the
dead and seated Him at His right hand in the heavenly places, far above all principality and power
and might and dominion, and every name that is
named, not only in this age but also in that which is
to come. And He put all things under His feet, and
gave Him to be head over all things to the church.

—Ephesians 1:16-22

Woe to you who plunder, though you have not been
plundered;
And you who deal treacherously, though they have
not dealt treacherously with you!
When you cease plundering,
You will be plundered;
When you make an end of dealing treacherously,

They will deal treacherously with you.

O LORD, be gracious to us;

We have waited for You.

Be their arm every morning,

Our salvation also in the time of trouble.

At the noise of the tumult the people shall flee;

When You lift Yourself up, the nations shall be scattered;

And Your plunder shall be gathered

Like the gathering of the caterpillar;

As the running to and fro of locusts,

He shall run upon them.

The Lord is exalted, for He dwells on high;

He has filled Zion with justice and righteousness.

Wisdom and knowledge will be the stability of your times,

And the strength of salvation;

The fear of the Lord is His treasure.

—Isaiah 33:1-6

The LORD is good,

A stronghold in the day of trouble;

And He knows those who trust in Him.

But with an overflowing flood

He will make an utter end of its place,

And darkness will pursue His enemies.

What do you conspire against the LORD?

He will make an utter end of it.

Affliction will not rise up a second time.

For while tangled like thorns,

And while drunken like drunkards,

They shall be devoured like stubble fully dried.

From you comes forth one

Who plots evil against the LORD,

A wicked counselor.

—Nahum 1:7-11

...for I will give you a mouth and wisdom which all your adversaries will not be able to contradict or resist.

—Luke 21:15

Working of the Blood of Jesus

Pray for the release of authority, power and peace through the blood of Jesus. There is redemption, and you are made perfect in the blood of the everlasting covenant. Pray that your conscience be cleansed with the blood of Jesus, and that you receive a multitude of grace and peace. Cover the doorposts of your house and cover your possessions with the blood of Jesus.

Decree:

> ...and by Him to reconcile all things to Himself, by Him, whether things on earth or things in heaven, having made peace through the blood of His cross.
>
> —Colossians 1:20

> In Him we have redemption through His blood, the forgiveness of sins, according to the riches of His grace...
>
> —Ephesians 1:7

Now may the God of peace who brought up our Lord Jesus from the dead, that great Shepherd of the sheep, through the blood of the everlasting covenant, make you complete in every good work to do His will, working in you what is well pleasing in His sight, through Jesus Christ, to whom be glory forever and ever. Amen.

—Hebrews 13:20-21

...how much more shall the blood of Christ, who through the eternal Spirit offered Himself without spot to God, cleanse your conscience from dead works to serve the living God?

—Hebrews 9:14

...elect according to the foreknowledge of God the Father, in sanctification of the Spirit, for obedience and sprinkling of the blood of Jesus Christ:
Grace to you and peace be multiplied.

—1 Peter 1:2

> Now the blood shall be a sign for you on the houses where you are. And when I see the blood, I will pass over you; and the plague shall not be on you to destroy you when I strike the land of Egypt.
>
> —Exodus 12:13

Courage, Boldness, and Might Against the Enemy
Pray for courage and that you would be strong in the Lord and in the power of His might.

Decree:

> This Book of the Law shall not depart from your mouth, but you shall meditate in it day and night, that you may observe to do according to all that is written in it. For then you will make your way prosperous, and then you will have good success.
>
> —Joshua 1:8

> Finally, my brethren, be strong in the Lord and in the power of His might.
>
> —Ephesians 6:10

Releasing the Power of God

Psalm 35:1 says that God will contend with those who contend with us. He will fight for you and ensure the enemy meets his demise. Who is this King of glory? The Lord strong and mighty, The Lord mighty in battle (see Psalm 24:8).

Decree:

> O Lord God, to whom vengeance belongs—
> O God, to whom vengeance belongs, shine forth!
> That You may give him rest from the days of adversity,
> sity,
> Until the pit is dug for the wicked.
>
> —Psalm 94:1, 13

> Save me, O God, by Your name,
> And vindicate me by Your strength.
>
> —Psalm 54:1

There they are in great fear
Where no fear was,
For God has scattered the bones of him who en-
camps against you;
You have put them to shame,
Because God has despised them.

—Psalm 53:5

He frustrates the devices of the crafty,
So that their hands cannot carry out their plans.
He catches the wise in their own craftiness,
And the counsel of the cunning comes quickly
upon them.
They meet with darkness in the daytime,
And grope at noontime as in the night.

—Job 5:12-14

Blessed be the LORD my Rock,
Who trains my hands for war,
And my fingers for battle—
My lovingkindness and my fortress,
My high tower and my deliverer,

My shield and the One in whom I take refuge,

Who subdues my people under me.

—Psalm 144:1-2

Angelic Assistance

Ask God to release the angels of the Lord to assist you as you fight. He can engage Michael, the warring angel, and the mighty army of heaven, to fight your enemies.

Decree:

"Behold, I send an Angel before you to keep you in the way and to bring you into the place which I have prepared."

—Exodus 23:20

To such as keep His covenant,

And to those who remember His commandments to do them.

The LORD has established His throne in heaven,

And His kingdom rules over all.

Bless the LORD, you His angels,

Who excel in strength, who do His word,

Heeding the voice of His word.

Bless the LORD, all you His hosts,

You ministers of His, who do His pleasure.

Bless the LORD, all His works,

In all places of His dominion.

Bless the LORD, O my soul!

—Psalm 103:18-22

But to which of the angels has He ever said:

"Sit at My right hand,

Till I make Your enemies Your footstool"?

Are they not all ministering spirits sent forth to minister for those who will inherit salvation?

—Hebrews 1:13-14

Then he said to me, "Do not fear, Daniel, for from the first day that you set your heart to understand, and to humble yourself before your God, your words were heard; and I have come because of your words. But the prince of the kingdom of Persia withstood me twenty-one days; and behold, Michael, one of the chief princes, came to help me, for I had been left alone there with the kings of Persia."

—Daniel 10:12-13

Zebulun is a people who jeopardized their lives to
the point of death,
Naphtali also, on the heights of the battlefield.
The kings came and fought,
Then the kings of Canaan fought
In Taanach, by the waters of Megiddo;
They took no spoils of silver.
They fought from the heavens;
The stars from their courses fought against Sisera.

—Judges 5:18-20

And when the servant of the man of God arose ear-
ly and went out, there was an army, surrounding
the city with horses and chariots. And his servant
said to him,
"Alas, my master! What shall we do?"
So he answered, "Do not fear, for those who are
with us are more than those who are with them."

> And Elisha prayed, and said, "LORD, I pray, open his eyes that he may see."
>
> Then the LORD opened the eyes of the young man, and he saw. And behold, the mountain was full of horses and chariots of fire all around Elisha.
>
> So when the Syrians came down to him, Elisha prayed to the LORD, and said, "Strike this people, I pray, with blindness." And He struck them with blindness according to the word of Elisha.
>
> —2 Kings 6:15-18

Battling Against Demonic Forces

Loose battering rams against demonic gates of hell set against us. Bind demonic oppressors who seek after our souls. Pray that the angel of the Lord pours fire from heaven upon our enemies. Pray that the devices of Satan, the accuser of the brethren, be frustrated and cast down.

Decree:

> In his right hand is the divination for Jerusalem: to set up battering rams, to call for a slaughter, to lift the voice with shouting, to set battering rams

against the gates, to heap up a siege mound, and to
build a wall.

—Ezekiel 21:22

Lay siege against it, build a siege wall against it, and
heap up a mound against it; set camps against it
also, and place battering rams against it all around.

—Ezekiel 4:2

For strangers have risen up against me,
And oppressors have sought after my life;
They have not set God before them.
Selah

—Psalm 54:3

Destroy, O Lord, and divide their tongues,
For I have seen violence and strife in the city.

—Psalm 55:9

As he loved cursing, so let it come to him;
As he did not delight in blessing, so let it be far
from him.

As he clothed himself with cursing as with his garment,
So let it enter his body like water,
And like oil into his bones.
Let it be to him like the garment which covers him,
And for a belt with which he girds himself continually.
Let this be the LORD's reward to my accusers,
And to those who speak evil against my person.

—Psalm 109:17-20

Then another angel, having a golden censer, came and stood at the altar. He was given much incense, that he should offer it with the prayers of all the saints upon the golden altar which was before the throne. And the smoke of the incense, with the prayers of the saints, ascended before God from the angel's hand. Then the angel took the censer, filled it with fire from the altar, and threw it to the earth. And there were noises, thunderings, lightnings, and an earthquake.

—Revelation 8:3-5

He frustrates the devices of the crafty,
So that their hands cannot carry out their plans.
He catches the wise in their own craftiness,
And the counsel of the cunning comes quickly upon them.
They meet with darkness in the daytime,
And grope at noontime as in the night.

—Job 5:12-14

Then I heard a loud voice saying in heaven, "Now salvation, and strength, and the kingdom of our God, and the power of His Christ have come, for the accuser of our brethren, who accused them before our God day and night, has been cast down."

—Revelation 12:10

PRAYER FOR SALVATION

I acknowledge that Jesus Christ is God; that He came into the earth as a sinless man. I am thankful that He died in my place and paid the price for my sin. I repent and confess that I have lived for myself and not obeyed God. For He made Jesus, who knew no sin, to be sin for me so that I might become the righteousness of God in Him. He was in the beginning with God. All things were made through Him, and without Him nothing was made that was made. Jesus, I believe that You died on the cross, were put in the grave, and on the third day, resurrected from the dead. Father, I know that I have sinned and it has separated me from you. Please forgive me. I now invite Jesus to come into my heart. Lord, take up residence and begin living and reigning through me. I am ready to trust Jesus Christ as my Lord and Savior. I confess with my mouth and believe in my heart the Lord Jesus, and that He was raised from the dead. I thank you that I am saved. Father, send your Holy Spirit and fill me up. In Jesus' name, Amen.

NOTES

INTRODUCTION

1.	"Strateia," Bible Hub, Strong's Concordance, accessed October 1, 2019, https://biblehub.com/greek/4752.htm.

CHAPTER 1: ESTABLISHING YOUR FOUNDATION FOR SPIRITUAL WARFARE

1.	Stew Smith, "Military Boot Camp At A Glance," military.com, accessed October 29, 2019, https://www.military.com/join-armed-forces/military-basic-training-boot-camp.html.

2.	Deployable Training Division, Joint Staff J7, "Insights and Best Practices Focus Paper: Authorities, Second Edition," jcs.mil, October 2016, accessed January 9, 2020, https://www.jcs.mil/Portals/36/Documents/Doctrine/fp/authorities_fp.pdf.

3.	"Harpazo," Bible Hub, Strong's Concordance, accessed October 14, 2019 https://biblehub.com/str/greek/725.htm.

CHAPTER 2: WEAPONS OF WAR: PRAYER AND INTERCESSION

1.	Adela Just, "Prayer and Intercession," generals.org,

October 14, 2014, accessed December 6, 2019, https://www.generals.org/articles/single/prayer-and-intercession/.

2.	"Penuel," Bible Study Tools, Easton's Bible Dictionary, accessed January 10, 2020, https://www.biblestudytools.com/dictionary/penuel/.

3.	"Tselem," Bible Study Tools, Strong's Concordance, accessed October 1, 2019 https://www.biblestudytools.com/lexicons/hebrew/nas/tselem.html.

4.	"Mishael," Bible Study Tools, Easton's Bible Dictionary, accessed October 1, 2019, https://www.biblestudytools.com/dictionary/mishael/.

5.	"Paga," Bible Study Tools, The NAS Old Testament Hebrew Lexicon, October 1, 2019, https://www.biblestudytools.com/lexicons/hebrew/nas/paga.html.

CHAPTER 3: CONFIGURING YOUR WEAPONS

1.	"M16A2 5.56 Rifle," military.com, accessed January 9, 2020, https://www.military.com/equipment/m16a2-556-rifle.

2.	The Editors of the Encyclopaedia Britannica, "Gunsight, Firearms," brittanica.com, July 20, 1998, accessed January 9, 2020, https://www.britannica.com/technology/gunsight.

3.	"Midian," Bible Study Tools, Easton's Bible Dictionary, accessed January 22, 2020, https://www.biblestudytools.com/dictionary/midian/.

CHAPTER 4: KNOW YOUR ENEMY

1.	"Cherubim," Bible Hub, ATS Bible Dictionary, accessed January 15, 2020, https://biblehub.com/topical/c/cherub.htm.

2.	Don Stewart, "What Are the Three Heavens?" blueletterbible.org, accessed December 14, 2019, https://www.blueletterbible.org/faq/don_stewart/don_stewart_151.cfm.

CHAPTER 5: PREPARING FOR BATTLE

1.	Ronald E. Goodman, "Strategy and Tactics, Military," scholastic.com, accessed January 9, 2020, https://www.scholastic.com/teachers/articles/teaching-content/strategy-and-tactics-military/.